Christm

A Double Bill of Festive Poems

ex libris

Candlestick Press

Published by:

Candlestick Press,
Diversity House, 72 Nottingham Road, Arnold, Nottingham NG5 6LF
www.candlestickpress.co.uk

Design and typesetting by Craig Twigg

Printed by Ratcliff & Roper Print Group, Nottinghamshire, UK

Cover illustration © Melissa Lhoirit, 2021
www.meligraphics.com

Candlestick Press monogram © Barbara Shaw, 2008

© Candlestick Press, 2021

ISBN 978 1 913627 01 0

Acknowledgements

Thanks are due to the authors listed below for kind permission to use their poems,
all of which are published here for the first time:

Andre Bagoo, Panya Banjoko, Geraldine Clarkson, Jonathan Edwards, Katherine
Gallagher, Matthew Hedley Stoppard, Stephen Keeler, Nick Makoha, Lorraine
Mariner, Rob Miles, Jessica Mookherjee, Cheryl Moskowitz, James Nash,
Bethany W Pope, Jacqueline Saphra, Tom Sastry, Clare Shaw, Penelope Shuttle,
Gregory Woods and Holly Yuille.

Contents

Cut

Who are you, when you watch this one?
No one is ever really the audience
when the screen powers on, and the house lights
flicker off, one by one. Are you the parent
who falls to the floor before your child
has been quite baked to completion? Are you
Little Girl Lost, looking for romance,
finding white snow and a palmful of blood?
Maybe you're the horny next door neighbor,
you know, with the bouffant hair and ill-
fitting pants? But no. Nobody comes
to this film to feel unfulfilled. Nobody
chooses the most-likely role for their
longed-for sessions of pretend. I know
exactly who you are. Listen: you're
watching this at Christmas, all alone.
You've got a *Nightmare Before...* mug filled,
to the brim, with wine you bought at Lidl.
You're watching a thin Tim Burton stand-in
carving sculptures with his fingernails
while his one True Love grows slowly old
in the village down below, and you're thinking
of the person you'd want to be with tonight,
sharing your blanket, if they'd only call,
if they'd take your scissor-hands in theirs.
That's who you are, who you always are,
and it's why you'll keep the lights down low
and watch it again.

Bethany W Pope

Christmas Day in San Francisco

A day of Bay Area cold and mist on Sherman Street
in a room borrowed from a friend, son of a
South African dentist who signed his letters,
'Floss well'. His sister couldn't make it, so I took
the bed instead, spent too much time indoors
and wrote poems on sadness. *Gone with the Wind*
was the Christmas film at The Castro, empty but
for a few unpartnered men. I chose the biggest box
of popcorn and put it on the seat next to me like a friend.
In those days I wasn't eating, so the popcorn stayed
untouched while Scarlett scowled on the screen with
her thirteen-inch waist, mine pretty much the same,
and everyone else's names disappearing in the credits.

Cheryl Moskowitz

The Chronicles of Narnia

Somewhere, there's another world
behind a door you've been knocking on
since you were young.

It's not that you want to escape your life –
just that somewhere, very close by,
in a room you've never explored,

there's a forest where snow falls
in the warm light cast by a lamp.
The moon hangs in a clear Northern sky,

the stream is frozen.
There are thousands and thousands of stars.
You don't need a key, or a ring

and there's no point in knocking:
every heart is a secret door.
One day, you'll walk right through

and you'll be there.
Perhaps a shadow in the trees will approach you.
You'll feel powerful and brave and very small.

Then your heart will be lion and mountains,
an acre of blue flowers blooming
and you'll stride into a world

you've always believed in
because there was always a river
and bright moss and birdsong

and stars – oh my love
though I didn't know how to reach you
all my life, I knew you were there.

Clare Shaw

Drifting

By the time the lion roared
twice we could nearly hear it –
outside the window
a sparkle, almost a feather,
fell and stuck to the earth.

A shimmering flap of wing,
and while the chiselled actor
started the long drive home,
and the mulled wine sank in our throats,
outside, the world was covered
in icing sugar, thin and sweet.

Just when he met the girl
who worked at the holiday shop
and coaxed him, so serious, to skate on the ice,
outside, out there, the white was up to the gate latch
and children were rolling a snowball
the size of a beach ball
up and down the empty road.

Around the point we paused for popcorn
and clicked the heat on,
and said *how dark it's got,*
we turned our backs on
the layer of cold settling high on the
outside of the glass.

At last when he learned
the true meaning of Christmas
and kissed the girl and saved the day
and came out quite new in his ugly festive jumper,
I was pretending I hadn't been crying
and you were shaking the blanket off and
outside, just outside, they were digging tunnels,
from the houses at the top of our road all the way down to the Cathedral
and above it all, the night sky
kept snowing.

Holly Yuille

The Methodists' Christmas Party

Wide miles across the polished ice we trudged
that night, and under passing yellow gas
lamps, high above our straggling band;

fresh cinders had been scattered on the road
– a pencil drawing etched in grit – and in
toy boots and duffel coats and gloves

we were hot-milk-and-malted-biscuit warm,
and stumbled up the shovelled roadside snow
and down again the other side

like crossing wintered continents.

We passed O'Toole's, the butchers, dark and locked
– no dog tied to the railings, or a bike
or pram outside – already faint

in muted memory, bleached blue against
the moon. The sudden chapel, square and black
as if it had been hewn from coal.

An open door leaked thin unheated light;
a screen set up where Sunday school should be;
the same cold seats against cold legs;

and other children's fathers, shirt sleeves rolled,
in careless party hats and shiny hair;
and someone switched off all the lights

and loud, and scratched as ancient glass

and flickering, black-and-white, and tooting down
a megaphone of motes of lighted dust
was *Steamboat Willie's* Noah's Ark

about to break a deluge where I sat
pinned back against the rising surf. Upstairs
I heard the ladies making tea.

Stephen Keeler

"Mistletoe can be deadly if you eat it –"
"but a kiss can be even deadlier, if you mean it…"

This memory returns like a batarang
that's knocked a crook unconscious:
seeing Pfeiffer pin Keaton's wrists
to the snow beneath her high heels
then lick him chin to nose –
even at 11, already a casualty
of two divorces, able to elude adults
in a cloud of cigarette smoke,
I realised there's someone for each of us
no matter how damaged we become.

During our first Christmas together
I saw in your eyes the same
hypnotic spiral, The Penguin
spinning his opened umbrella,
and over a dozen Christmases down
the line, sparks still fly when we kiss
like Catwoman bringing a taser to the lips,
using her eighth life to cremate
Christopher Walken and be free of her curse.

Matthew Hedley Stoppard

Basquiat asks the Poet about Death on Christmas Eve

At a rooftop party, the night is the night, and we are watching death.
Or should I say Bruce Willis is walking barefoot in a skyscraper? I wish
I had taken a picture. The host, some news caster you would recognise
from TV, has hired a firm to project the film onto the hotel wall across
the street. My date has just returned from the bathroom. I am her plus
one. Pointing to the open bar, I can feel the sun's heat reflecting off
the building. She has me speaking in my fourth language but my thoughts
have us undressed in my first. By the pool a waiter asks *Are you ready*
to order? You recommend the pad Thai with chicken for two and
if they are out of that you say we will go for the snapper with a snake
bean salad. DJ Shadow is connecting speakers to his decks when
his left elbow knocks the Blood Orange Champagne Mule to the concrete.
Even falling has its grace. Bruce Willis is at the top of the Nakatomi building
ready to face a paradox – terrorists intend to blow it up – a building burning
is a way of saying - you're not welcome here. The waiter returns with our
cutlery – I can see my country in the steel with only weeks to go before
it is bankrupt. As if one needed the reminder of how I can be in two places
                                                                    at once.

Nick Makoha

Meet Me in St Louis!

The little council house always seemed filled
with snowlight at that time. I always had *Heidi*
hugged hardback to me, with shiny Alpine cover.
Split grapefruits, sugared after Midnight Mass
the night before, on the table for once-yearly
breakfast treats. The front room, where the TV
was: a focus, but so small, you had to get in early,
trick or squeeze to get a seat; kids usually ended up
on the floor. Dad had his seat, Mum was usually still
'finishing off' in the kitchen…

                    'Meet Me in St Louis!'
Now, years later, and after many lockdowns
(meeting no one *anywhere*), I watch it alone,
taking a sip of Canton Ginger Liqueur… Savouring
the brash carnival opening credits; the greetings card
tableau which quickens into the first vignette:
a season, a poem – like stepping inside
a doll's house when it flickers to life….
Family members appear, taking it in turns
to sing and hum the title song; come and go,
offering opinions over a bright copper pot
of simmering ketchup. The airy rooms – chandeliered,
gilded, gold-oak-panelled – are so different
from ours. And a family of girls, not boys. Margaret O'Brien,
a tot – 'Tootie' – funnelling all that suppressed middle-class
white angst, subverting it to firecrackery outrageousness:
Poor Margaretha… she has four fatal diseases!… It'll take me at least
a week to dig up all my dolls from the cemetery… Wasn't I lucky
to be born in my favourite city!… I'm the most horrible!
I take another sip of ginger.

                              Maybe a love affair –
behind the scenes – between Garland and Minnelli, the Director…?
Primped, flounced, ruffled costumes, puff-sleeved, wasp-waisted,
delicious: ice-cream slacks for the men, and boaters…

Enough wit and salt and wiles to offset schmaltz.
This peanut heart cracks open
a little. It's the music. The strain of melancholy,
like the spirit in Baileys Irish Cream, running through.
Have Yourself a Merry Little Christmas –
the song Sinatra animated with seasonal magic,
replacing the wartime 'we'll have to muddle through
somehow' with 'hang a shining star upon the highest bough'.
Wisps of instrumental, half-recognised, *Down at the Old*
Bull & Bush, Auld Lang Syne... 'Time goes by but we'll be together...'
Ah, they did well, to keep together...

                                        ...and to stay in the family home!
We lose our homes so easily... Good that there's always one
more to come back to: this (pistachio!) (walnut!) heart –
a nugget, like amber, encompassing all the remembered folks
and times, in one sublime sunlit kernel. Permapresent...
A ginger-peachy show... The final scene: the glittering
lagoon paradise of the St Louis World's Fair,
and Judy in the midst of her family marvelling
that this most *breathtaking*, this most *beautiful*, is
'Right here, where we *live! *Right *here in St Louis!*'

Geraldine Clarkson

A Brief History of Watching *A Christmas Carol*

So all of us lined up here in a room,
the sofa doing what it does – be soft –
and on the screen some bloke is being Scrooge
again, the latest brand new version of
                    the same old dude.

Sometimes he's counting coins, haranguing Bob
in black-and-white, sometimes he lifts or lugs
a technicolour child star Tiny Tim,
who's famed years later for his Hollywood-
                    sized love of drugs,

sometimes he's dancing in his dressing gown
through snow that's not snow really, and sometimes
he's singing songs which fill our heads and rhyme
badly. Sometimes he flies through the night sky
                    in CGI,

and sometimes he's the posh and skull-haired one
we know from *Star Trek*, phasers set to stun,
trained on the Ghost of Christmas Yet to Come.
Sometimes he is a night-capped Michael Caine
                    with mutton chops,

discussing his romantic life or soul
with Kermit the Frog. Each version works again
to how he screws up his entire life,
and then he starts out giving people stuff
                    and puts it right.

Here on the sofa, in the Christmas lights'
flashing glow, we're watching memories
of what we watched before, or what we'll see
some version of next Christmas, or the next.
                    And suddenly

I think of all those mirrors at the barber's,
the way they stretch away, in front, behind,
forever, reproduce themselves again,
again, and how they flash and offer now
                    perhaps, this view:

beyond the piles of hair, the hairdryers,
beyond the Saturday girl sweeping up
the afternoon, right here now, stepping forward
in his slippers, Albert Finney, is it,
                    breathing in,

then cartwheeling the length of the whole room.

Jonathan Edwards

When Love is Gone

The toddlers were restless at the test screening
during the number where Belle breaks her engagement
to Scrooge, so the executives ordered it cut.

Along with my sisters, I watched Michael Caine out-humbug
Britain's finest Shakespearean actors annually on VHS,
where the song remained intact, so couldn't believe

it didn't actually feature the first time we left the Odeon,
our hearts brimming with Muppet joy, and joined the concrete
of Romford's shopping precinct, December 1992.

Having now witnessed my niece belting Frozen's 'Let it Go',
tapping into 36 months of grievances, I know that feelings
run deep for toddlers. Scrooge has never seemed more isolated.

Jacob Marley becomes Marley & Marley, the cantankerous
balcony hecklers perfectly cast, even Gonzo's Charles Dickens
gets a sidekick in Rizzo the Rat, and all our Muppet dreams come true;

Kermit and Miss Piggy as Bob and Emily Cratchit are married
and happily, and boy does Kermit need Miss Piggy's sass
to get by in Victorian London. Those executives were wrong.

Even toddlers can benefit from a puppet-free moment to pause
and reflect on an ungenerous life, as we begin Scrooge's transformation
from miser to a man who knew how to keep Christmas,

Caine singing for the first time in his career – trying to join in
with his pure-voiced lost love, missing the notes and breaking down,
as she warns us all, "I wish you well but I must leave you now, alone."

Lorraine Mariner

Thanks for the Wings: Ode to *It's a Wonderful Life*

Don't mourn, I can be unborn if that will stop this gloom.
I can untie myself from the rope used to haul the moon

inside my mother. I'm a luminous flux, the drench
light from her fingertips. The paintings are on my wall.

You saw God in galleries, thought artists were greater
than you, yet they couldn't paint your light. Average man;

teeter on the brink before you jump to make an angel.
I'm that bridge, second rate; grown of odds, sods and debts.

I'd unmake this unwinged body, in a second, untie knots,
to keep my rose petals in your pocket. Reap kindness.

If you were not-born, not my flying carpet from Samarkand
made of fairy tales, if darkness doesn't shine the universe,

if the Christmas film we watch is simply a trick of light,
then stars we claim are mere space dust, not this guiding myth

that appears on each station, each Christmas, in endless repeat.
Our story is kindness; grow your wings. It matters how it ends.

Jessica Mookherjee

Love Actually

One

It seems to be a film of floppy hair
Of missed chances and a kind of London rush,
A whirl of images, (not sure I care)
From Downing Street to Shepherd's Bush.
Bum notes are struck, and it's not a sin,
Like the Quality Streets that no one wants,
A scatter of characters left in the tin,
Foil-covered Guildenstern and Rosencrantz.
But then the moments that pierce your heart
Of pure emotion quite unconfected
And I forgive the film its lack of art,
And the odd simper I have detected.
For all its swagger and occasional fails
I salute the brave pilgrims in these Tales.

Two

Metropolitan stories quite tangled,
A box of decorations and lights
Where the glitter's worn, the fairy mangled
They might struggle to sparkle these dark nights.
Childhood has gone, quite irretrievably,
Sometimes feels as if it has never been,
And with it my dreams of a perfect tree
Its piney, Christmas hug of evergreen.
But love can be remade, be found again,
Goodbyes become helloes, new baubles put on show,
Let's string up the lights, and try to regain
Some courage in their intermittent glow.
As loss is sharpened, let your hope expand,
And love actually might take your hand.

James Nash

The Holiday

Here is a plot that holds no jeopardy, the sweet win-win.
It turns you soft, it holds you helpless as it reels you in:

see Iris weep the night away, trying not to fall apart
before she heads to Hollywood to fix her broken heart.

Behold Amanda fly across the pond, then drag her pain
on wheels, her case of unshed tears, along an icy English lane.

O, blessed tropes of British snow and California sun!
I sink into the cushions as you put the kettle on.

We know the score, we fall into the safety of the story;
we watch on – partly for the truth but mostly for the glory

and indeed, the plot unfolds the way that we expect:
the peril's mild, love blooms, there's no explicit sex.

We unwind, sip our Christmas blend and live the dream:
love's triumph floating softly to the top like cream.

We wait: the music swells, and then – surprise, surprise!
Iris learns to laugh again; and finally, Amanda cries.

Loved up, lit up, each holds her power and her man;
the New Year rises to the task, extends a velvet hand

and leads them to the dance. You stroke my head,
I kiss your lips and arm in arm, we wander off to bed.

Jacqueline Saphra

A Plot for Keeps

Bridget knew no lonely years were ever quite the same –
she wanted changes, a life that wasn't always tame:
Christmas with her mother's turkey curry, clumsy thinking,
mumsy-gaffes about Mark Darcy – Bridget's smoking drinking
would never win him. *As if she cared.* She saw his sharp disdain,
the very thing to put her off. She'd start a diary again:
resolves, find a nice man, quit cigarettes, wine, lose pounds
be wise and intellectual, forget those office hounds,
stop flirting with Daniel Cleaver, ignore him. Too bad
he was her boss, she'd thought he loved her. O Bridget, sad,
and Darcy, ubiquitous, indeed, always asking why
she was with this Daniel oaf: *he himself, liked her, truly.*

The challenge between Daniel and Mark became more set,
but Bridget, funny girl, bunny-girl, hadn't seen it yet:
the diary's moments, new TV job, becoming famous,
her birthday party – things turning fabulous.
With Darcy dropping by to save the day, the meal at least;
everyone happy till Daniel arrived, ruined the feast –
got himself almost killed by Bridget's new knight,
proud Mr Darcy, who left in shame and anger. Such a fight!
As for Bridget, all by herself again, *Had she lost Mark forever?*
Well, she'd told Daniel she wanted *extraordinaire*, not him. Ever.

The plot again: another party, she heard Mark was due to go
to New York. *It mustn't be*, she thought. *No, no,*
she spoke her heart, let Mark see that Daniel *had* gone ...
But the plot said, *Too soon yet*, a Christmas in Paris was on,
très bon. But, Bridget wasn't going, for 'Mr Wonder' Mark
arrived, not gone to New York, how her heart sang in its dark –

until, upstairs, she saw he'd read her diary crits of him, and left. O no,
love never ran unsmooth as this . . . Half-dressed, out into the snow,
she caught him, told him the diary wasn't true. He said it was a start,
he'd bought her a new one. And Bridget, joy in her heart,
knew this year wasn't like those others in the past.
This was a plot for keeps. She and Mark – together at last.

Katherine Gallagher

Joyeux Noël

A man in the trenches
cradles his mum's alarm clock.

The Crown Prinz attends the opera,
a prudent distance from the guns.

Christmas Eve 1914. Snow falls.
A piper blares softly.

A row of Christmas trees
along the German lines. Lit candles.

Silent night. Stille Nacht.

After the singing,
a kickabout in no-man's land.

Gifts of booze and baccy exchanged.
Buttons, hats, chocolate.

Icy stars over the battlefield
and the unburied dead.

No two armies ever this close,
and for so long a duration.

Wakeful, homesick,
one man unhasps

the pearl-handled penknife
his wife gave him.

Useful for prising open tins,
paring nails, peeling fruit.

Shivering over the blade,
he hears its steely promise.

'I will take you home to Kate
and the girls, Alfred, not a scratch on you.'

Penelope Shuttle

The boys get away in the end

It's Christmas and there are bones in the kitchen,
not enough seats. Our sofa
is comfortable for two. *Sit here*
between us it says.
The film is *The Sting*. Two hours
of Robert Redford
whose famously desirable presence
allows the drinking aunts
to show us boys
they know all about desire.
The cringe was paid for, in advance
with roast potatoes and postal orders:
if we aren't grateful we know we should be
and that keeps us quiet.
Anyway, it's not for long. Soon
the Vauxhalls will be crawling up
the lesser arteries of the road network
back to Yorkshire and Norfolk, reviewing
every mouthful, every word.
The sofa leans forward. I'm pressed in the middle.
It's this moment I remember
when it's my turn to consider
how a smaller body feels.
Redford is running from the sergeant
who wants a piece of what he and Paul Newman
are up to. His feet start landing
on invisible keys
picking out the melody of *The Entertainer*
and the danger
dissolves.

It's all just a performance
from which Redford, Newman
even the demonic Robert Shaw
probably emerged with smiles
to be other things, on other days, to other people.

Tom Sastry

Stillness

By lunch on the day, the heavy lifting's done:
Carcass in the fridge, pans put in to soak,
   The formal extortion of fun
Abandoned like a corny cracker joke
Binned with the paper and glittering twine.
Mother and I at peace, the truce has held,
     Its irritations quelled
By all but the lees of our bottle of wine.
The rest of the festival stretches ahead
Across a desolate tundra of TV ordeals
     Until merciful bed.
Of the pleasures on offer nothing appeals,
Nothing to go with our coffee and Marsala –
Or nothing but something called *Dersu Uzala.*
     What could be cheerier –
'A Kurosawa masterpiece on universal themes'
     Set in Siberia,
A native hunter's broken spoken Russian
   Subtitled into broken written
English? (Enough to give Mother concussion.)
And yet, by some miracle, soon we were smitten,
   Involved, inveigled, entranced, enraptured –
Although a captive audience, happy to be captured…
     Impassive as the ancient hunter's face,
      The seasons passed at glacial pace.

In the teeth of their extremes,
From seething summer silence to a howling Arctic wind,
    The plot didn't thicken, it thinned:
Men move across the landscape and grow closer to each other
        Until one dies. The end.
    With nothing to say of it, Mother
  And I, we shared a smile, no discord to defend.
  Familial love is an uncompromising illness,
Its agitations only ever reconciled by stillness.

Gregory Woods

The Stopover

Draw the curtains, crank the boiler up some more,
nail the knitted draught excluder to the door,
fetch woollen throws to swaddle our knees,
expel the gloom of dusk and misplace the keys.

Prepare for an assault of homemade pies,
spiced pears, butterscotch sauce, and satisfied sighs.
Chuck squabbles out the window, suspend disbelief,
if loneliness rears its head charge towards relief.

You are the venom on my ancient tongue
for man or woman bold enough to do you wrong,
the reason for my aches, the dog-tiredness of my sleep,
my blood, my bone, my heart, the rhythm in me deep.

Turn the telly up, *The Snowman's* nearly on,
let's take this time to walk on air, for the future belongs to none,
when you return to your domain, with gift and sloppy kiss
remember always this: I'll be mourning, and you'll be missed.

Panya Banjoko

Good Grief
after *A Charlie Brown Christmas* (1965)

My hand came down fast. I hadn't quite grasped
the true meaning of Christmas.
We'd been watching Charlie Brown deal with Lucy improvising
psychiatry, Sally's avarice, even Snoopy *gone commercial.*

Classmates either side concurred, the movie's central message came
when Linus van Pelt stepped out to tell
the King James version of the story – and by some miracle, letting go
of his infamous comfort blanket.

But I also wanted to discuss Charlie's praise of Pig-Pen's dust
*... the soil of some great past civilisation. Maybe
the soil of ancient Babylon. He may be carrying soil
trod upon by Solomon. Or even Nebuchadnezzar...* my fascination, truth

be known, for that awkward kid, witnessed from the wings rehearsing
'Christmas Time Is Here' for our musical – brilliant specks
drifting from his duffle in the spotlight, rising
all around him like rewinding snow.

Rob Miles

A Movie Whose Title We've Long Forgotten

Shows on the television set that has been moved aside to the corner of the room where we children huddle around it while parents lime in the drawing room sipping ponche a crème and rum. The same movie was on the previous year when we visited Aunty B in Paramin and the steep ascent of the road was like parang music, jolting us above the mist as players pranced from house to house decked in green, gold, and red. It was the claymation one, the movie, the one with Rudolph and the Abominable Snow Monster and the Island of Misfit Toys, you remember it, right? It was on TTT the year we stayed up late to go to midnight mass, the house smelling of ham and sweetbread while someone outside burst bamboo, the one in which something was forever happening, some story involving antlers budding from bright hair and Santa's misfit elves running away, and just as their pudding bodies were fixed yet molten clay, so too our lamb-like selves are glued to the screen, each frame savoured the way a pastelle filled with meat and olives is sliced and eaten, the way a poem is read line by line, as adults perfume themselves in other rooms while poinsettias bleed glorious red wine and we become drunk on the sense of repetition, the sense of an unending procession of scenes following what came before, what comes next: reindeer flying, stars like tinsel, a bright red nose, a Latin mass, incense rising, an altar with pieces that move as the wicked monster falls into a white chasm of ice. And Rudolph is not flawed, not weak, his bright red difference is his immaculate strength and soft horns have become a crown that will be worn, like a beloved silver brooch, each year, each time, again and again so that we may remember that Christmas Eve and the laughter on the hill.

Andre Bagoo